Greenwillow
Read-alone

HELEN R. HADDAD

Truck and Loader

pictures by DONALD CARRICK

GREENWILLOW BOOKS · New York

THIS STORY IS FOR GEORGE
—H. R. H.

FOR RUSTY
—D. C.

Text copyright © 1982 by Helen R. Haddad
Illustrations copyright © 1982 by Donald Carrick
Printed in U.S.A.   First Edition   10 9 8 7 6 5 4 3 2 1

Library of Congress Cataloging in Publication Data

Haddad, Helen R.   Truck and loader.
(Greenwillow read-alone books)
Summary: Truck and loader, working together,
help to build roads, remove trees, and dam a
pond for a swimming pool with a sandy beach.
1. Dump trucks–Juvenile literature.
2. Loaders (Machines)–Juvenile literature.
[1. Dump trucks 2. Loaders (Machines)
3. Trucks. 4. Machinery] I. Carrick, Donald, ill.
II. Title. III. Series.
TL230.H25   629.2'24   81-6823
ISBN 0-688-00826-7   AACR2
ISBN 0-688-00827-5 (lib. bdg.)

CONTENTS

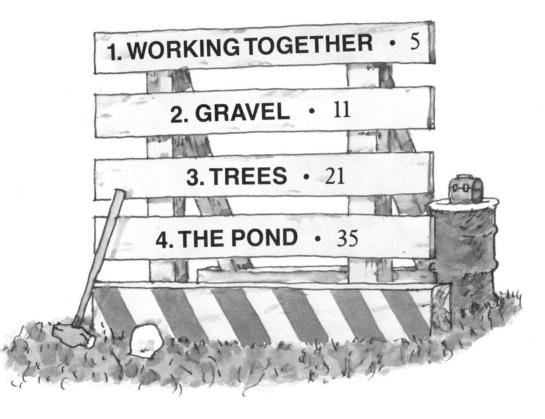

J35299

A dump truck comes rumbling

down the road

to the gravel pit.

The truck has a big dumper.

It can carry a heavy load.

But the dump truck
cannot load itself.
A big, noisy front-end loader
is waiting
by a pile of gravel.
The loader has a scoop
on the front end.
The scoop is used
to load things.

The front-end loader
and the dump truck
make a good team.
They work together
to get a job done.

The truck and loader

can move sand,

gravel, and stones.

They can clean up leaves,

clear snow,

and help fix streets.

They can load and dump

almost anything.

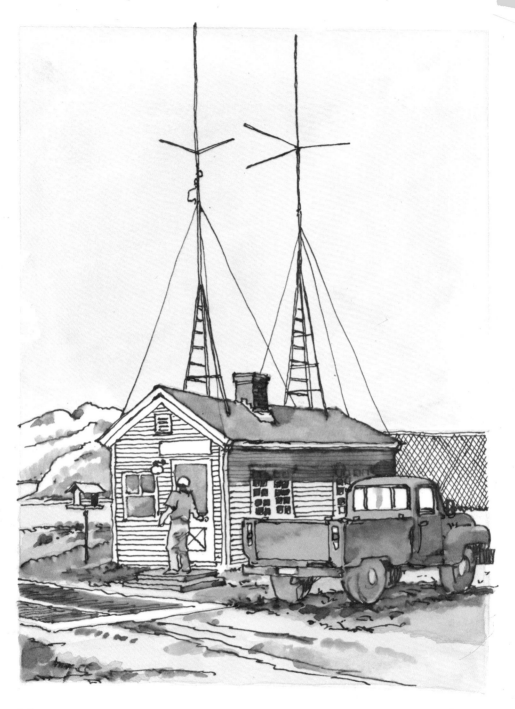

The loader and the truck

are ready to work.

A road builder

comes to the gravel pit.

He asks for twenty truckloads

of gravel.

"See you at the roadbed,"

says the road builder.

11

The driver starts the loader.

He makes the loader

dig its scoop

into the gravel.

The scoop lifts up

full of gravel.

The driver turns the loader.

Now the scoop

is over the truck's dumper.

The driver makes

the scoop tip down.

The gravel showers

out of the scoop

and into the dumper.

But the dumper is not full.

The truck's dumper

is much bigger

than the loader's scoop.

Dig, scoop, lift, and tip.

Dig, scoop, lift, and tip.

Soon the dumper is full.

"See you later,"

says the truck driver.

He drives the truck away.

"Over here,"
says the road builder.
He shows the truck driver
where he needs the gravel.

"Not in a pile," he says.
"Spread it out, please."

The road builder opens

the tailgate on the dumper.

The driver starts the truck moving.

He pulls a lever

to tip the dumper up.

The gravel pours out

onto the roadbed.

The truck keeps moving.

When the dumper is empty,

the driver stops the truck.

"Well done,"

says the road builder.

All day the driver

makes the loader scoop gravel

into the dump truck.

The truck goes back and forth,

back and forth,

from the gravel pit

to the roadbed.

Twenty loads of gravel

are spread on the roadbed.

"Good job,"

says the road builder.

**3.
TREES**

"This tree is dead,"

says the tree man.

"It must be taken down.

The loader and the dump truck

can help."

The loader is near the tree.

"Want a lift?"

calls the driver.

The tree man climbs

into the loader's scoop.

He is lifted up

to the branches of the tree.

His helper throws a rope

up over a high branch.

The tree man ties the rope around

the branch to be cut

with his chainsaw.

Then the branch is

lowered to the ground.

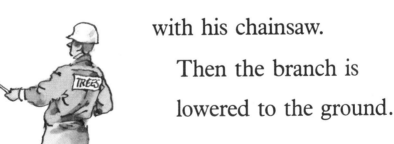

J35299

Only the trunk is still standing.

The tree man cuts a notch

on one side of the trunk.

The sawdust flies out.

Then he cuts through the trunk
from the other side.
The trunk crashes down.

The branches and the trunk
are cut and split into firewood.
"Load the truck,"
shouts the tree man.

The wood is piled

into the loader's scoop.

The scoop is lifted

over the dump truck.

The logs clunk into the dumper.

The dump truck looks

like a woodshed.

The truck takes
all the wood away.
The firewood will keep
a house warm in winter.
Where the tree grew,
only a low stump
and some sawdust are left.
The tree man says,
"We must plant a new tree."

The truck driver takes the truck
to get the new tree.
When the truck has gone,
the tree man says,
"Let's get the hole ready."
He and his helper
work to dig a hole.

The truck comes back.
"Here's the tree,
and it's a big one,"
calls the truck driver.

"Coming,"

shouts the loader's driver.

He puts the loader's scoop

even with the tailgate.

The men slide the tree

into the scoop.

The tree is carried in the scoop
and then lowered into the hole.
"Hold it," shouts the tree man.
They slide the tree
out of the scoop.

Carefully the driver
makes the scoop push the dirt
around the new tree.
"Good work,"
says the tree man.

4. THE POND

"I want a small pond
to swim and fish in,"
says Mrs. Teri.

"I have a little brook.
The loader can widen
and deepen the brook,"
she says.

"Then it can build a dam.

And to make the pond

I will need

the dump truck too."

"You want the pond right here?"
asks the loader's driver.
"Yes, right there,"
answers Mrs. Teri.

The driver makes the loader

scoop out dirt and stones.

It loads them

into the dump truck.

The truck driver takes
the dirt and stones
to fill a low spot
near Mrs. Teri's house.
The truck makes
many trips back and forth.

Now there is a big, muddy place
where the loader is digging.
"Make it wider and
a little deeper, please," says Mrs. Teri.
So the driver makes the loader
dig the hole wider and deeper.
The dump truck takes away
a load of mud.

Mrs. Teri looks at
the wide, deep muddy hole.
But the place still
doesn't look
like a pond.

The driver takes the loader
to the low end of the hole.
He will make the loader
push and pile dirt and stones
to build a thick wall.

Now there is a dam
at the low end of the hole.
Water from the little brook
flows into the pond.

The water gets higher and higher
behind the dam.
Now there is a pond.

When the pond is full,

the water will spill

over the dam and

go on down the brook.

The loader's scoop
is very muddy.
The driver makes the loader
put its scoop into the water
to wash out the mud.
He lifts up the scoop
full of water.
A waterfall pours out.

Mrs. Teri looks at the pond.
"Now we need some sand,"
she says.
"I want a nice sandy beach."

"We'll get some sand,"

says the truck driver.

The loader and the truck

are driven to the sand pit.

Dig, scoop, lift, and tip.

Soon the dumper

is full of sand.

"See you later,"

says the truck driver.

He drives back to the pond.

The sand is spread
at the pond's edge
to make a beach.

"Now the pond is just right,"
says Mrs. Teri.
"What a good job."

The dump truck rumbles off
to join the loader.
They are ready
for another job.

DONALD CARRICK began illustrating this
book just as a truck and loader started digging up
his street! He has collaborated with his wife, Carol,
on such popular books as *The Empty Squirrel,*
A Rabbit for Easter, and *Paul's Christmas Birthday.*
He is the author-artist of *Harold and the Giant*
Knight and *The Deer in the Pasture.* The Carricks
and their two sons live on Martha's Vineyard
and spend their summers in Vermont.

HELEN R. HADDAD was born in Boston,
Massachusetts. She received an A.B. in history from
Smith College, attended the School of the Boston
Museum of Fine Arts, and later did graduate
work in Art, Education and Child Study at Smith.
She is the author-artist of *Potato Printing* and the
illustrator of *Centennial Cuisine,* a cookbook.
She lives with her husband and four children in
Northampton, Massachusetts.